THE G.I. SERIES

Gulf War
Desert Shield and Desert Storm, 1990–1991

Front cover: Corporal Robert C. Unhoch, of the 1st Battalion, 2nd Marines, surveys the area after arriving at his mission location during Exercise 'Imminent Thunder', part of Operation 'Desert Shield'. The marine is armed with an M16A2 rifle which has the M203 grenade launcher attached to the underpart of the rifle. He is clad in daytime desert camouflage BDUs, known to G.I.s as 'chocolate chips', with the desert field-pack cover which is designed to camouflage the olive-green All Purpose Lightweight Individual Carrying Equipment (ALICE). He wears a Kevlar helmet, nicknamed the 'Fritz' helmet, with its desert camouflaged cover and has a pair of oversized desert goggles to protect his eyes from sand-blown storms or helicopter rotor blade wash.

Four Star General Norman Schwarzkopf, Commander-in-Chief, U.S. Central Command, smiles for the camera during a visit to Kuwait in the aftermath of Operation 'Desert Storm'. He is wearing a daytime desert camouflage battledress uniform (BDU). Note the subdued Combat Infantry Badge and Master Parachutist Badge.

THE G.I. SERIES

THE ILLUSTRATED HISTORY OF THE AMERICAN SOLDIER, HIS UNIFORM AND HIS EQUIPMENT

Gulf War
Desert Shield and Desert Storm, 1990–1991

Anthony A. Evans

Greenhill Books
LONDON
Stackpole Books
PENNSYLVANIA

Greenhill Books

Gulf War
first published 2003 by Greenhill Books, Lionel
Leventhal Limited, Park House, 1 Russell Gardens,
London NW11 9NN
www.greenhillbooks.com
and
Stackpole Books, 5067 Ritter Road, Mechanicsburg,
PA 17055, USA

British Library Cataloguing in Publication Data

Evans, Anthony A.
The Gulf War: Desert Shield and Desert Storm,
1990–1991. – (The G.I. series: the illustrated history
of the American soldier, his uniform and his
equipment; v.29)
1. United States. Army–Equipment 2. United States.
Army–Uniforms 3. United States.
Army–History–Persian Gulf War, 1991 4. United
States. Army–History–Operation Desert Shield,
1990–1991 5. Persian Gulf War, 1991 – Participation,
American 6. Operation Desert Shield, 1990–1991 –
Participition, American
I. Title
956.7'0442373

ISBN 1-85367-533-4

Library of Congress Cataloging-in-Publication Data
available

All photographs in this book are courtesy of the
United States Department of Defence

Designed by David Gibbons, DAG Publications Ltd
Layout by Anthony A. Evans, DAG Publications Ltd
Printed in China

JUN 0 1 2011

GULF WAR
DESERT SHIELD AND DESERT STORM, 1990–1991

On 2 August 1990, Iraq invaded its neighbour Kuwait, which led to a furious international reaction and, less than six months later, a very destructive war.

Disputed oil fields at Rumailla on the Kuwait–Iraq border were the main and overt cause of the invasion. Iraq's leader, Saddam Hussein, demanded rights to the oil fields, but he also knew that control of Kuwait's coastline would give Iraq greater and more convenient access to the Persian (or Arabian) Gulf. The West was caught napping, and was at a great strategic and psychological disadvantage during the first weeks following the Iraqi–Kuwait confrontation.

The U.N. Security Council condemned Iraq's invasion, urged a cease-fire and demanded a withdrawal. Instead, Iraq strengthened its hold over Kuwait, and the U.N. mounted Operation 'Desert Shield' to prevent any further Iraqi aggression, especially against Saudi Arabia. Rapidly deployed from the U.S.A. and Europe, the G.I.s were to head the international Coalition forces. The Commander-in-Chief was American Lieutenant General H. Norman Schwarzkopf.

On 7 August 1990 the 2,300-strong 'Ready Brigade' of the U.S. 82nd Airborne Division loaded HUMVEES and a handful of Sheridan light tanks into transport planes at Pope Air Force Base for a flight to Dhahran, Saudi Arabia.

A few days later, on 12 August, leading elements of the 7th MEB (Marine Expeditionary Brigade) boarded C-141s for the first of 250 flights to transport the whole Brigade to Al Jubail, Saudi Arabia, from California. By 25 August the 7th MEB was 15,000 strong, with 123 tanks and 425 various pieces of artillery. It moved north the 200 miles to the Saudi–Kuwaiti border. On 26 August, elements of the Hawaii-based 1st MEB also began landing at Al Jubail.

By both air and sea the massive build-up of U.S. units created the most spectacular of the Coalition forces commited to Desert Shield. Troops and equipment were drawn from U.S. VII Corps stationed in Germany as well as from units stationed in the U.S.A.

By 30 August the American commitment in the Gulf and Saudi Arabia had risen to 260,000 men. European and Arab–Islamic forces totalled nearly 200,000. Iraq countered by moving 545,000 troops, 4,300 tanks, 2,700 armored personnel carriers and 3,000 artillery pieces into the Kuwaiti theatre.

By November the U.S. XVIII Airborne Corps had reached its full strength of 118,000, with 28,000 vehicles, of which 5,000 were tracked, and 1,000 helicopters. VII Corps had 140,000 personnel, 43,000 vehicles and 7,000 tracked vehicles.

'Desert Shield' was succeeded on 16 January 1991 by 'Desert Storm', the code name for the Coalition campaign to eject Iraqi forces from Kuwait. At the start of 'Desert Storm' the Coalition was at an overall disadvantage of 2:3 in troop numbers and 1:2 in combat soldiers, as well as being outnumbered when it came to tanks and artillery. The American Commander-in-Chief and his staff concluded that they could compensate for their inferiority in numbers on the ground by the superior training of the U.S. forces and their superior equipment such as the M1A1 Abrams tank, the M2 Bradley IFV (Infantry Fighting Vehicle) and the AH-64 Apache attack helicopter.

The enemy had supposedly been on maximum alert for several days, but the U.N. air armada and cruise missile attacks achieved almost complete surprise. Around the clock, Coalition aircraft pounded targets inside Iraq and Kuwait, targeting bridges, command posts, communication centres, troop concentrations and artillery emplacements. A major effort was made to hit the SCUD missile sites, as the Iraqis tried to hit back the only way they could by firing SCUDs against Israel, Saudi Arabia and the Gulf states which were within range.

The air campaign began at midnight on 16/17 January 1991. On 29 January an Iraqi attack on Al-Wafra was the prelude to an advance by the Iraqi Army into Saudi Arabia and the Battle at Khafji. The offensive was carried out by three Iraqi Brigades from their 5th Mechanised Infantry Division. The Iraqi columns failed to get anywhere near their objectives, suffering heavy blows at the hands of the U.S. Marines and being particularly hurt by the Marines' TOW anti-tank missiles. One column did manage to get into Khafji, despite losing most of its supporting tanks to a Qatari unit equipped with French-built AMX-30 tanks. Marines, Saudi and Qatari forces launched a counter-attack on the town and the Iraqis surrendered. The poor Iraqi performance was to be an indicator of their general lack of professionalism throughout the conflict.

On 24 February Schwarzkopf commenced the ground war along a 270 mile (430-km) front. The Coalition armies began the offensive in Saudi Arabia. On the left flank of the Coalition's deployment was the XVIII Airborne Corps, which included a French light armoured division. U.S. VII Corps, including the British 1st Armoured Division, was to their right, occupying the central position. Even further right were the U.S. 1st and 2nd Marine Divisions, with the combined brigades of Egypt, Syria, Saudi Arabia, Kuwait and Oman, together with Qatari/United Arab Emirates units.

The plan envisaged a ground offensive designed to trap and eliminate Iraqi forces inside the KTO (Kuwait Theater of Operations). On the left the XVIII Airborne Corps – consisting of the U.S. 82nd and 101st Airborne Divisions, the U.S. 24th Infantry Division (Mechanized), the U.S. 3rd Armored Cavalry Regiment and the French 6th Light Armoured Division (*Division Daguet*) – was to strike north into Iraq and the Euphrates valley in order to protect the Coalition's western flank and to cut off a potential escape route for the Iraqi Army. VII Corps would also move north into Iraq, but then turn east to take the Iraqi reserves in the flank. Meanwhile, the two

Marine divisions and the Arab units were to advance north straight into Kuwait itself.

This offensive began on 24 February, as planned, with a direct attack towards Kuwait City on the right (east) and the outflanking moves in the centre and on the left (west). The XVIII Airborne Corps' strike was carried out nearly 300 miles to the west and beyond the notice of Iraqi observers. The first part of this Corps' plan was for the *Division Daguet* with support from elements of the 82nd Airborne Division to cover the far left and for the 101st Airborne Division (Air Assault), to sweep around the Iraqi defences (the 'Saddam Line'), isolating the KTO and securing the left flank. The 101st Airborne Division succeeded in mounting what has been described as the largest airmobile operation in military history, utilising some 300 helicopters to transport 2,000 troops and establish a Forward Operating Base (FOB 'Cobra') 70 miles inside Iraqi territory. The French *Division Daguet* also reached their first objective. Iraqi resistance was minimal with XVIII Corps suffering only one man wounded.

In the centre, led by the the U.S. 1st Infantry Division and spearheaded by 1,300 tanks and nearly 6,000 tracked vehicles, the 140,000-strong VII Corps – the largest and strongest armoured corps in the history of battle – opened up more than a dozen breaches in the Iraqis' formidable defences. Through the gap they established poured a screening force, the U.S. 2nd Armored Cavalry Regiment, followed by the British 1st Armoured Division, whose job was to safeguard the right flank of VII Corps. Also the U.S. 1st and 3rd Armored Divisions, which would provide the main punching force of VII Corps, rolled into Iraq.

The troops facing Kuwait on the right flank, with the M60 tanks and Cobra gunship helicopters of the Marines, cut through the Iraqi defences. With their accompanying Arab Allies, they shattered four Iraqi infantry divisions and by the end of the day had secured Al-Jeb airfield.

On day two of the ground offensive, 25 February, the weather conditions deteriorated. Sandstorms reduced the visibility to 30 yards. The Iraqis could not compete with the Allies' night fighting and foul weather capabilities. So, despite the conditions, most Allied commanders knew where they were and in what direction they were going, all with the aid of global positioning satellites (GPS) systems.

The *Division Daguet* continued to advance on the extreme left of the Coalition line, proceeding to take Al-Salman airfield, 70 miles inside Iraq, by nightfall. To its right, the 101st had carried out an air-assault overnight to cut the Bagdad to Basra highway and establish Area of Operations (AO) 'Eagle'. The 101st also consolidated their position in the Euphates valley during the afternoon. To the east of the 101st, the 24th U.S. Infantry Division advanced 60 miles into Iraqi territory without managing to meet a single Iraqi soldier.

To their right, VII Corps was making good progress. That morning the 1st U.S. Infantry Division, having consolidated the bridgehead, let more forces of VII Corps through the breaches in the Saddam Line. As planned, the 1st and 3rd U.S. Armored Divisions and their screening force of the 2nd Armored Cavalry Regiment made major advances into enemy territory, easily brushing any Iraqi forces aside as they moved forward. Also during that afternoon and night the British 1st Armoured Division, on VII Corps eastern flank, engaged and smashed the Iraqi 12th Armoured Division.

Having consolidated their bridgehead on the eastern flank, the Pan-Arab and Marine units came up against some Iraqi armoured resistance, with a counterattack being mounted initially against the U.S. 2nd Marine Division. This turned out to be one of the Iraqis' most costly ventures: they were heavily defeated by the Marines. Iraqi armoured units sent against the 1st Marines suffered much the same fate. All the Iraqi forces that stood in the way of these two Marine Divisions and the 1st ('Tiger') Brigade of the U.S. 2nd Armored Division fell prey to the Americans firepower. At the end of the day, the Coalition's right wing was only ten miles short of Kuwait City.

Day three of the offensive dawned with the *Division Daguet* and the 82nd secure on the western flank against any Iraqi units sent against them.

The XVIII Airborne Corps continued to strengthen its hold on the Euphates valley, with the 101st making helicopter air assaults against the enemy. The 24th Infantry Division had, by evening, continued to make good progress and then turned east towards Basra, with its attack helicopters in the lead. They ran into an Iraqi brigade of T-72 tanks attempting to flee. It was annihilated by the U.S. force, losing all of its 50 or more Russian-built battle tanks in the process.

In the centre, VII Corps was closing on the Iraqi theatre reserve, which contained the much-vaunted Iraqi Republican Guard. The 2nd Armored Cavalry managed to make initial contact with Republican Guard forces late in the day. Although high winds caused poor visibility in the desert, the 1st and 3rd Armored Divisions moved closer to delivering the fatal blow to the Republican Guard. During the day, elements of the XVIII Airborne Corps and VII Corps fought the Iraqis in what, some have said, was the largest tank battle in history.

In the meantime, the British 1st Armoured Division, after completing the destruction of the Iraqi 12th Armoured Division, then pushed aside units of two more Iraqi Armoured Divisions. In the course of the fighting to date, the British had destroyed over 250 enemy armoured vehicles. Then, along with the U.S. 1st Infantry Division, they reached their objectives and extended their lines.

The U.S. 1st Cavalry Division, an armored division, had now passed through the breach in the Saddam Line and was moving north-west to join the forthcoming battle.

An Iraqi counterattack by their 3rd Armoured Division was carried out against the U.S. 1st Marines Division at Kuwait Airport. The Iraqis were unable to inflict any serious casualties on the American troops and the Marines easily defeated this tank attack. It was reported that more than 250 knocked-out Iraqi tanks and 70 other armoured vehicles were counted in the region of the airport after the battle. The Arab and Marines forces were now set to enter Kuwait City, putting the last of the Iraqis to flight as the city fell into the hands of Kuwaiti fighters.

By the end of the fourth day much of the Iraqi Army had been routed. The previous night, the U.S. 1st and 3rd Armored Divisions, the 24th Infantry Division and the 101st Airborne Division had begun the final fight with the Republican Guard, the battle lasting all day and on into day five. VII Corps accounted for three of the Guard's best divisions. The tougher of the Guard units did put up a stubborn fight, but, as the American armour moved forward, the Coalition overwhelmed the Iraqis. Some of the U.S. forces even called off air support during the night engagements, as they feared there might be more Allied casualties through 'friendly fire' than Iraqi return fire.

Trapped by the Coalition's encircling movements, the Iraqi armies were completely defeated within 100 hours. Washington decided to declare an end to the fighting, apparently influenced by media reports of the 'Highway to Hell', the destruction of Iraqi men and vehicles during their retreat to Basra. By now Iraqi resistance in Kuwait had ceased. But the cease-fire meant that hundreds of Iraqi tanks and more than 1,000 other armoured vehicles managed to escape the Coalition net. The cease-fire came into effect on 28 February 1991.

In over four days of continuous movement and combat VII Corps achieved particularly good results while fighting some of the better units of Saddam's army. They reported destroying an estimated 1,300 enemy tanks, 1,200 armoured personnel carriers and fighting vehicles, nearly 300 artillery pieces and capturing approximately 22,000 Iraqi troops during the battle. The corps itself had suffered extremely light casualties in both men and combat vehicles.

Coalition forces were to continue to reduce the number of Iraqi units during occasional clashes which took place after the cease-fire. The largest occurred on 2 March, when units of the U.S. 24th Infantry Division retaliated against a Republican Guard column which had opened fire on them while the Iraqis were attempting to escape north into Iraq.

The use of overwhelming firepower and speed were the keys to the Allied victory, which saw the destruction of at least the equivalent of two dozen Iraqi divisions. Of the 500,000 or more American personnel deployed during 'Desert Shield' and 'Desert Storm', losses totalled 160 killed, some accidentally, and 457 wounded. Other Allied casualties were 77 killed and 830 wounded. Iraqi casualties are indeterminate; they could have totalled as many as 100,000 killed and 300,000 wounded.

Saddam's army had been the fourth largest in the world at the start of the war. Its huge tank inventory included the Russian T-72 tanks, which were mostly fielded by the Republican Guard. These were slightly more modern than the U.S. Marine Corp's M60s, but many of the Iraqi tanks were older types, such as the T-54/55s, T-62s and Chinese built T-59/69s. Most of the American tanks were the M1A1 Abrams. A 'high-tech' tank, the Abrams was fitted with excellent night and foul-weather fighting capabilities, a superb 120mm gun and a first-rate powerpack. Technically, it was a whole generation ahead of the T-72. The Iraqi artillery, which had acquired a fairly good reputation during the course of its eight-year war with Iran, managed to inflict only minimal casualties on the Coalition forces. The Coalition artillery and air bombardments either destroyed most of the Iraqi guns or forced the gunners to abandon their weapons. One captured Iraqi artillery officer revealed that of the 100 guns with which he started the war, twenty were knocked out by the Allies' air attacks, but only seven remained after they were subjected to the artillery barrages laid down by the Allied ground forces.

In professionalism, both in combat and logistically, the American G.I.s proved they had no match. Their equipment, on the whole, proved to be among the best in the world, particularly the magnificent M1A1 Abrams tank. Above all, the war had shown what can be achieved, no matter what the odds, by properly trained and motivated volunteer soldiers, who believe in what they are doing.

'Courage Conquers' is the motto of the 1st Battalion of the 37th Armor Regiment, U.S. 1st Armored Division. As Colonel Dyer, the commander, so rightly says, 'The soldiers performed magnificently and they all certainly lived up to our battalion's motto.'

FOR FURTHER READING

Dinackus, Thomas D. *Order of Battle: The Ground Forces in Operation Desert Storm.* Hellgate Press, 2000

Michaels, G. J. *Tip of the Spear: U.S. Marine Light Armor in the Gulf War.* Naval Institute Press, 1998.

Pilmott, John and Badsey, Stephen (editors). *The Gulf War Assessed.* Arms and Armour Press, 1992.

Scales, Robert H. *Certain Victory: The U.S. Army in the Gulf War.* AUSA Institute/Brassey's, 1998.

Schwarzkopf, General H. Norman and Petre, Peter. *It Doesn't take a Hero.* Bantam Books, 1992.

Vernon, Alex, Creighton Jr, Neal and McCaffrey, Barry R. *The Eyes of Orion: Five Tank Lieutenants in the Persian Gulf War.* Kent State University Press, 1999.

Right: Members of the 1st Battalion, 325th Airborne Infantry Regiment, wearing daytime desert camouflage BDUs, cut their way through concertina wire defences during a live fire demonstration in Saudi Arabia.

Below: M1A1 Abrams main battle tanks of Company A, 3rd Battalion, 32nd Armored Regiment, 1st Cavalry Division test their guns prior to taking part in an exercise during the Operation 'Desert Shield' deployment in Saudi Arabia.

Above: Corporal Childs, Headquarters Company, 7th Marines is wearing a desert pattern 'Boonie Hat' and standard daytime camouflage BDUs. He is setting up an 60mm M224 mortar during Operation Desert Shield. In addition to a high-explosive bomb this weapon fires the full range of 60mm bombs, including phosphorus and illumination bombs.

Right: The M2 Bradley IFV (Infantry Fighting Vehicle) has a crew of three and can carry six fully equipped combat troops into battle at a speed in excess of 40mph. It is armed with a 25mm Chain Gun in a two-man turret and two TOW (Tube-launched, Optically-tracked, Wire-guided) anti-tank guided weapons as well as a 7.62mm coaxial machine-gun. The Bradleys proved to be extremely effective in supporting armoured and infantry units during 'Desert Storm'.

Right: An ammunition specialist of the 1st Cavalry Division, as denoted by his shoulder insignia, carries a 105mm Armour Piercing, Discarding Sabot round, to be used in an M1 Abrams MBT (Main Battle Tank) during 'Desert Shield'. Over 500 M1s were initially deployed in the Gulf region but were subsquently replaced by M1A1s transferred from Europe. The M1A1 Abrams is equipped with the more powerful 120mm main gun. The badge on the G.I.'s left shoulder is that of the 1st Cavalry Division.

Above: An M1A1 Abrams MBT (Main Battle Tank) laying a smoke screen. With its 120mm main gun firing a wide range of ammunition, the M1A1 dominated the tank battles of 'Desert Storm'. Even when Iraqi T-72 tanks were hiding in hull-down positions behind five-foot thick ramparts of sand, the M1A1's APFSDS-T (Armour Piercing, fin Stabilised, Discarding Sabot-Tracer) rounds could blast straight through the sand and still destroy the T-72s. As reported in the Army Times a sergeant of D Company, 1st Battalion, 35th Armor said that at 2,800 meters his unit engaged some enemy tanks and watched as an Iraqi tank turret flew some 40 feet into the air when the tank exploded when hit. He was amazed by the amount of firepower his tank had and how much destruction he could do. It was a sobering thought.

Opposite page, top: Two marines from the 3rd Remotely Piloted Vehicle (RPV) Platoon prepare a Pioneer RPV for launch during Operation Shield. The Iraqi soldiers eventually became so demoralised that on occasions some tried to surrender to these remotely controlled aircraft.

Right: Marine artillerymen from the I Marine Expeditionary Force fire their M198 155mm howitzer in support of the opening of the ground offensive to free Kuwait during Operation 'Desert Storm'. The M198 performed well during Gulf operations. With rocket-assisted shells, the M198 has a maximum range in excess of 30,000 yards. The Coalition artillery played an influential part in the fighting to retake Kuwait from the Iraqis.

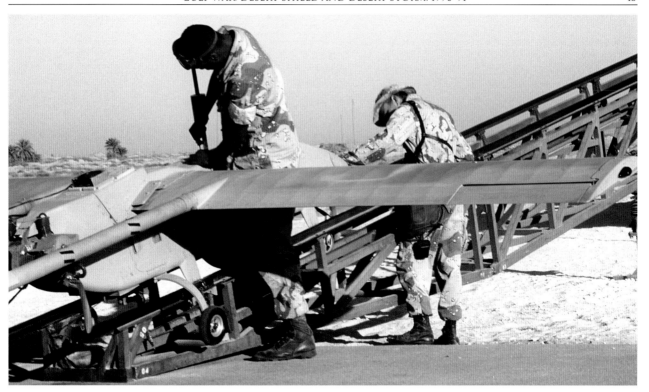

Left: Two Marines man a Mark 19 grenade launcher as they guard the headquarters of the 3rd Marine Regiment. The launcher is equipped with a night vision scope. The Mark 19 is a tripod-mounted rapid fire weapon which fires 40mm calibre grenades.

Right: Personnel of Battery C, 21st Air Defense Artillery, 11th Air Defense Brigade deploy an MIM-23B Hawk anti-aircraft missile system. Ageing and being replaced by the Patriot, the Hawk was still an effective weapon with a range of over 40,000 yards, a high supersonic speed and a hefty warhead.

Below: Members of the 1st Platoon, Company D, 2nd Amphibious Assault Battalion, 2nd Marine Division remove camouflage netting from a AAV7A1 amphibious assault vehicle while taking part in a training exercise during 'Desert Shield'. Intended for landing troops on open beaches, the AAV7A1 is scaled to be seaworthy and is a bulky amphibious tracked vehicle. The capacious troop compartment can hold up to 25 marines or four and a half tons of supplies.

Right: A helicopter crewman from the 101st Airborne Division (Air Assault) stands beside an AH-64A Apache helicopter as it is prepared for takeoff. The helicopter is armed with a M230A1 30mm automatic Chain Gun beneath its cockpit and is carrying sixteen AGM-114 Hellfire missiles on its wing pylons. Apaches fired the first shots of the war when, as a prelude to the main air attacks, they destroyed Iraqi radar sites to create a number of 'safe lanes' for Coalition aircraft to fly through.

U.S. marines roll into Kuwait International Airport in LAVs (Light Armored Vehicles) after the retreat of the Iraqi forces from Kuwait during 'Desert Storm'. This LAV is a MOWAG Piranha licence-produced by General Motors of Canada for the U.S. Marine Corps and the U.S. Army. The vehicle is loaded down with all the usual accoutrements of war and is only armed with a 7.62mm M240 machine-gun, indicating that it is either a recovery version of this vehicle or the supply-carrier variant.

Above: A company from the 101st Airborne Division (Air Assault) marches across the apron to board aircraft that will carry the unit to Saudi Arabia for Operation 'Desert Shield'. They are clad in daytime desert camouflage BDUs and lightweight jungle boots. They are all wearing their 'Fritz' Kevlar helmets, with a desert camouflage cover.

Right: The emblem of the 101st Airborne Division, the *Screaming Eagles*, is displayed prominently on the boarding stairway of the aircraft that will carry them to Saudi Arabia. The troop's kit has already been stowed in the hold of the aircraft; they only carry their M16A2 rifles. The 101st is an Air Assault Division and carries the word 'Airborne' in its title as an honourary designation denoting the division's past history as paratroopers.

Above: Marines waiting on the pier to board a ship for the Persian Gulf. They will be transported by U.S. Navy ships. Mobilisation for the Gulf War happened so quickly that the marines are still wearing the standard pattern BDUs rather than the desert pattern. The desert pattern BDUs were issued to them later. The marines are waiting with their equipment around them, but their M16A2 rifles have been stowed without magazines.

Opposite page, top: Loaded down with their gear, members of the 4th Marine Expeditionary Brigade (4th MEB) walk along the pier beside the amphibious transport docking ship USS *Shreveport* (LPD 12). The Marines of the 4th MEB were some of the first U.S. troops to be deployed to Saudi Arabia for Operation Desert Shield.

Right: In the background of the picture an M88A1 armoured recovery vehicle and an M1A1 Abrams MBT (Main Battle Tank) are off-loaded from a vehicle cargo ship during Operation Desert Shield. The M88A1 is a very successful variant of the venerable M48 MBT. These tanks have not yet been repainted in their desert camouflage colours.

Left: A crane lifts an M1A1 Abrams tank, weighing in at approximately 60 tons, from the freighter ship *Cape Mendocino* at a pier in the Persian Gulf. The *Cape Mendocino* was one of 60 ships activated from the Ready Reserve Force to serve during the Gulf War. The tanks have yet to be repainted in the desert colour scheme.

Right: M2A2 Bradley Infantry Fighting Vehicles about to be off-loaded from the *Maersk Constellation.* The 25mm Bushmaster guns have been removed from the turrets of these vehicles during their transit. The Bradley weighs some 22 tons and has a top speed of 40mph.

Left: An M1A1 Abrams MBT, being off-loaded from a civilian transport truck, arrives in the Persian Gulf. The tank has been repainted for desert operations. A frontline replacement for the older M1 tank, the M1A1 is fitted with several new features, including a multi-fuel gas turbine engine which gives it a high top speed of over 40mph.

Opposite page, top: A G.I. carries his gear away from the aircraft which has transported him to Saudi Arabia. His M16A2 is slung across his back as he shoulders his pack. He is wearing the daytime desert camouflage BDUs and matching covered 'Fritz' helmet.

Opposite page, bottom: Newly arrived Marines are led through an encampment near an airfield as they march through the desert for the first time. Apart from their M16A2 rifles, they are carrying the minimum of kit.

Below: Soldiers from the 82nd Airborne Division walk around their camp wearing NBC (Nuclear Biological and Chemical) suits, gloves and M17A1 protective masks as they try to acclimatise to the heat of the Saudi summer.

Left: A member of Battery A, 516th Air Defense Artillery Regiment, 11th Air Defense Artillery Brigade aims a Stinger Portable Anti-Aircraft missile launcher during Desert Shield. With an effective range of at least 3 miles, the supersonic missile has an infra-red seeker, and is capable of engaging low-altitude, high-speed aircraft and helicopters.

Opposite page: A M977 Heavy Expanded Mobility Tactical Truck (HEMTT) This family of vehicles is rapidly deployable and is designed to operate in any climatic condition where military operations are expected to occur and provides transport capabilities for re-supply for combat vehicles and weapons systems. There are five basic configurations of the HEMTT. The M977 cargo truck (as illustrated) with a Material Handling Crane (MHC) on its rear end, the 2500 gallon M978 fuel tanker, the M984 wrecker, the M983 tractor and the M985 cargo truck with MHC. A self-recovery winch is also available on certain models.

Below: An M163 Vulcan 20mm self-propelled anti-aircraft gun system travels with and escorts a convoy on a desert road during Desert Shield. The M163 consists of the ubiquitous M113 armoured personnel carrier married to a M61A1 Vulcan six-barrelled 20mm Gatling gun which is capable of firing up to 3,000 rounds a minute (50 per second).

Opposite page, top: A 5-ton M809 truck loaded with supplies. The M809 series was first built in 1960, and production continued for 30 years. Many are still in service with U.S. forces and there are several different variants of the basic truck. This cargo version is also often used as an artillery tractor.

Below: Members of the 1st Battalion, 325th Airborne Infantry Regiment, 82nd Airborne Infantry Division, armed with M16A2 rifles, clear a four-room 'Shoot house' made of tyres during an urban warfare, live-fire exercise during Desert Shield. They are wearing Personal Armor Systems for Ground Troops (PASGT) flak jackets over their BDUs.

Below: An M1A1 Abrams tank still in the standard European camouflage pattern. Many Abrams were taken from European stocks and when they reached the Gulf region they had not yet been repainted in a desert camouflage scheme.

Top left: A soldier of Company A, 3rd Battalion, 502nd Infantry Regiment, 101st Airborne Division runs for cover as he takes part in an urban warfare training exercise being staged in an abandoned town during 'Desert Shield'. Armed with an M16A2, he is wearing a desert pattern 'Boonie Hat' with standard daytime camouflage BDUs.

Left: Soldiers of Company A, 3rd Battalion, 502nd Infantry Regiment, 101st Airborne Division take part in an urban warfare training exercise in an abandoned town during Operation Desert Shield. The soldier in the foreground is armed with an 5.56mm M16A2 rifle while the other is carrying a 7.62mm M60 machine-gun which first appeared in

the late 1950s and went on to see extensive service during the Vietnam War. This venerable weapon has remained a platoon-level machine gun while the lighter Belgium-designed M249 is issued as the squad automatic weapon (SAW).

Above: Soldiers from Company B, 2nd Battalion, 8th Cavalry, receive instruction on the main armament used in the M1A1 Abrams MBT. This gun is a German-designed M256 Rheinmetall smoothbore 120mm and is also fitted to the German-designed Leopard 2 tank. It is probably the most effective tank gun in the world. During the course of Desert Storm this 120mm cannon was used effectively at ranges of over 3,500 yards, destroying huge numbers of Iraqi tanks.

Left: An ammunition specialist inspecting a 105mm Armour Piercing, Discarding Sabot round (APDS). This round consists of a core penetrator and a covering sleeve or 'Sabot'. The penetrator is made of either tungsten or depleted uranium; hard, dense, heavy materials which are ideal for punching a hole through the armour of an enemy tank. Such dense materials mean that the round would be too heavy if it was big enough to fill the barrel. So, the round is of smaller diameter than the calibre of the gun, which would normally mean that it would be weakly propelled and somewhat inaccurate. It is made up to the correct diameter by means of the lightweight Sabot, which has the sole purpose of filling the barrel and allowing the heavy core to be properly propelled, and thus reach a very high velocity and acceleration. The Sabot makes an air-tight fit in the barrel without significantly adding to the weight of the round. Upon firing, it applies the necessary 'squeeze', then falls off on leaving the muzzle.

Above: A member of the 1st Battalion, 325th Airborne Infantry Regiment instructs a Saudi Arabian Guardsman in the use of a Stinger AA missile launcher. The Stinger is being exhibited as part of an equipment and hardware display during Operation 'Desert Shield'.

Right: A member of the 1st Battalion, 325th Airborne Infantry Regiment prepares to load a 105mm shell into an M102 towed howitzer during an artillery demonstration for Saudi Arabian National Guardsmen. The M102 is used mainly by high mobility forces and airborne units. The gun weighs in at one and a half tons and is capable of throwing a rocket-assisted shell nearly ten miles.

Opposite page, top: Troops of the 3rd Battalion, 73rd Armor Regiment (Airborne), 82nd Airborne Division taking part in a training exercise during 'Desert Shield', preparing to move out to make an attack. The men all wear daytime desert camouflage uniform and lightweight jungle boots. The G.I. standing on the right has a AN/PRC-119 radio on his back.

Opposite page, bottom: A handful of 82nd Airborne Division M551A1 'Sheridan' light tanks were initially deployed for Operation 'Desert Shield'. During the Gulf War, the tank battalion of the 82nd was the only combat unit retaining the M551, which was mainly used for training purposes in the U.S.A., where they were driven by the

Opposing Force as 'enemy' tanks during combat training. Sheridans were armed with a unique 152mm gun/missile launcher which could fire both the Shillelagh guided anti-tank missile as well as more conventional rounds.

Above: An M551A1 Sheridan light tank of the 82nd Airborne Division, fully equipped with its supplies for war, waits to be loaded onto a C-130 Hercules transport aircraft. The Hercules is more than adequate for carrying this 17-ton tank. Even though the Sheridan is not as potent as an MBT (Main Battle Tank), it does have the one great advantage of being air portable, so it was one of the first armoured vehicles the U.S. was able to rush to Saudi Arabia.

Left: The M9 is a Beretta 9mm double-action semi-automatic pistol. Issued to replace the aging .45 calibre pistol, the 15-shot Beretta is carried by service members who do not carry rifles, such as tank crews and aviators.

Below: The M249 Squad Automatic Weapon (SAW). The SAW is a lightweight 5.56mm machine-gun carried by infantry squads. The SAW has the option of being fed by a 30-round magazine or a 200-round link-belt. Weighing fourteen pounds and with a combat range of 800 yards, the Belgium-designed SAW is one of the best weapons of its type anywhere in the world.

Above: The M47 Dragon is a one-man, shoulder-launched, short-range, wire-guided anti-tank/assault missile. The system made up of launcher, tracker and missile. The missile has a range of over 1,000 yards and is capable of knocking out most armoured vehicles and tanks. The launcher is expendable but the sights are not. The Dragon entered service in 1970 and has been upgraded and improved over the years.

Below: The M2HB Browning .50 calibre heavy machine-gun has been on the U.S. army inventory since 1933 and is still one of the best weapons in its class. It is mainly used as an anti-aircraft weapon and for providing sustained, heavy-calibre machine-gun support fire for ground units. The rate of fire can be adjusted from between 450 to 600 rounds per minute.

Above: M82A1 heavy-calibre, long-range sniper rifle. This 30 pound, .50 calibre weapon fires the same standard ammunition as the Browning .50 calibre heavy machine-gun. It has an eleven-round magazine. Not only can it be used against enemy troops, but it is also powerful enough to disable targets such as parked aircraft and radar dishes.

Left: The Swedish-designed AT-4 anti-tank weapon, called the M136 by the U.S., is a lightweight, expendable, self-contained, anti-tank rocket launcher. It can be operated by one man and has a maximum range of 300 yards. It was approved for service with the U.S. armed forces in 1985. A Marine corporal was awarded a Silver Star citation when, with no regard for his personnel safety, he grabbed an AT-4 and moved through automatic weapons fire and thick smoke to engage and single-handedly destroy an enemy tank that was attacking his position.

A marine riding a cross-country motorcycle, primarily used for courier work between units. The KLR 250 is a lightweight, rugged, commercial, cross-country motorcycle that has been modified for military use. As well as courier work, it is also used for reconnaissance and by the military police.

Opposite page, top: In the Gulf War the M109A3 was employed by both the U.S. Marines and the U.S. Army. It is an armoured, self-propelled, medium howitzer firing a 100-pound, 155mm shell to a range of twelve miles, and is used for indirect artillery support. The vehicle weighs some 25 tons, has a road range of 200 miles and is manned by a crew of six.

Opposite page, bottom: The M110A2 203mm (8inch) self-propelled howitzer can fire a 200-pound shell to a range of fifteen miles. This 30-ton unarmoured weapon is used for general, medium-range artillery support work. The vehicle road range is over 300 miles, and it is manned by a crew of five.

Above: The M270 Multiple Launch Rocket System (MLRS) is a free-flight artillery rocket system which made its combat debut during the Gulf War and proved to be a major success. It can ripple-fire its twelve rockets in less than one minute, the crewmen then quickly reloading the launcher with two six-pack pallets of rockets. The rockets have a maximum range of twenty miles, and each war-head contains 644 grenade-size sub-munitions which are scattered over an area more than half the size of a football field. Iraqi troops nicknamed them 'The Rain of Death'. The vehicle has a road range of 300 miles before it needs refueling and is manned by a crew of three.

Above: UH-60A Black Hawk medium lift helicopters prepare to take-off as the 82nd Aviation Brigade relocates in the desert. The Black Hawk is the U.S. Army's standard troop carrier. It has a flight crew of two, and accommodation in the main cabin for eleven fully equipped troops or six stretcher patients. It has a high cruising speed of 170mph. It can also be configured to carry Hellfire anti-tank missiles and rocket pods.

Opposite page, top: Two AH-64A Apache attack helicopters pass over the desert. These 150mph helicopters are armed with a pair of 19-round launchers for 2.75inch folding-fin rockets. The Apache to the right is also armed with eight AGM-114A Hellfire anti-armour missiles, four on each side.

Opposite page, bottom: An AH-64A Apache attack helicopter of the XVIII Airborne Corps, armed with sixteen AGM-114A Hellfire anti-tank missiles, is prepared for a mission.

Above: The 25mm Bushmaster Chain Gun is the primary armament of the Bradley IFV (Infantry Fighting Vehicle). The gun allows single-shot or automatic fire. It has dual-feed selection for either armour-piercing or high-explosive ammunition. The Bradley is also armed with a twin launcher for the TOW anti-tank missile, seen here on the nearside of the turret, and a 7.62mm coaxial machine-gun

Left: A corporal of Company C, 1st Battalion, 2nd Marines, armed with an M16A2 equipped with a M203 40mm grenade launcher on the underside of the barrel. He has a pair of desert goggles over his 'Fritz' helmet.

Above and below: The Chaparral provides mobile, short-range air defence against low-flying aircraft. The system consists of a heat-seeking missile, based on the Sidewinder air-to-air missile, modified for ground-to-air use. The missile is supersonic, has a range of 15,000 feet and an altitude of 10,000 feet. The fire unit is mounted on a M730 tracked vehicle which has a six-man crew and a top road speed of 40mph.

Above: Members of a mortar team from Company C., 1st Battalion, 2nd Marines, set up an 60mm M224 lightweight mortar. The fuse settings on the high-explosive round fired by the M224 can be set so that it will burst before impact, on impact or after impact. It also has snap-off propellant segments, allowing the gunner to vary the range by adjusting the amount of propellant.

Opposite page, top: The M60A1 AVLB (Armored Vehicle Launched Bridge) can launch and retrieve a 60-foot, scissor-type bridge. The bridge can be emplaced between two and

five minutes, depending on circumstances, and retrieved in less than ten minutes. The whole thing consists of three sections: the bridge, the launcher and the hull, which is based upon the M60 tank. It was used for bridging the wide anti-tank ditches that the Iraqis built as part of their defenses in the Kuwaiti theatre of operations.

Opposite page, bottom: Painted with a menacing shark's mouth, this LARC5 amphibious cargo-carrier of the Marine Corps crosses a beach during 'Desert Storm'.

Opposite page: The Abrams MBT has an unrefueled range of 300 miles and is powered by a 1,500hp multi-fuel gas turbine engine, giving the 57-ton tank a top speed of well over 30 miles per hour. It is armed with a 120mm high velocity gun and a coxially mounted 7.62mm machine-gun. It also has a .50 calibre anti-aircraft machine-gun and another 7.62mm machine-gun mounted on the turret top.

Above: 72nd Engineer Company, 24th Infantry Division test a mine-clearing rake attached to an M728 combat engineering vehicle. The M728 is based on the M60 tank, but is armed with a British-designed short-barrelled, 165mm demolition howitzer and is fitted with an A-frame jib boom, which is used for lifting and clearing obstacles. At the front of the vehicle there is also a dozer blade, to which the mine-clearing rake has been attached on this vehicle.

Left: A G.I. of the 34th Signal Battalion digs a foxhole at the new location of the 2nd Armored Cavalry regiment during 'Desert Storm'. The M820 van-bodied truck is a derivation of the M809 chassis type and carries a communications shelter. The inverted 'V' was painted on most Coalition vehicles as a friend-or-foe identification sign.

Opposite page: An Avenger air defence system. The Avenger consists of a four-tube Stinger anti-aircraft missile launcher mounted either side of an operator's station on a pedestal carried by an M998 HMMMV. A .50-calibre M3P machine gun can also be mounted beneath the right side of the Stinger launcher.

Above: Troops of Battery C, 1st Battalion, 319th Field Artillery Regiment, prepare an M102, 105mm howitzer for airlifting by a 2nd Battalion, 82nd Aviation Regiment, 82nd Airborne Division UH-60 Black Hawk helicopter.

Below: Attaching the gun to a hovering Black Hawk. The gun weight is one and a half tons, which the Black Hawk is more than capable of lifting.

Right: Airlifting two M102 howitzers. The 101st Airborne Division succeeded in mounting the largest wartime airmobile operation in combat history, utilising some 300 helicopters to transport 2,000 troops and their equipment, and establishing Forward Operating Base (FOB) 'Cobra' some 70 miles inside Iraqi territory.

Left: An M9 Armored Combat Earthmover (ACE) assigned to the I Marine Expeditionary Force moves towards the Kuwaiti border from Saudi Arabia at the start of the ground phase of Operation 'Desert Storm'. These vehicles proved very effective in destroying the Iraqi defensive trench systems.

Below left: A Marine, wearing a scrim-covered 'Fritz' Kevlar helmet, sights a target with his squad automatic weapon. Note his one-quart plastic canteen. The plastic canteen is prefered over the old metal ones, which would get hotter in the intense heat of Arabia.

Below: A member of the 101st Airborne Division cleans his M16A2 rifle while waiting for transportation to his duty station at the start of 'Desert Storm'. He is wearing the standard daytime camouflage BDUs. Attached to his All Purpose Lightweight Individual Carrying Equipment (ALICE) gear is an angle-headed flashlight.

Opposite page, top: A Senior Master Sergeant of the 4409th Explosive Ordnance Disposal Detachment examines the tail section of a SCUD missile supposed to have been shot down by an M1M Patriot air defence missile. The SCUD is a Soviet-designed battlefield support missile which is capable of carrying either a nuclear, a chemical/biological or a high-explosive warhead to a range of several hundreds of miles. SCUDs caused the Coalition serious concern and accounted for a number of lives during 'Desert Storm'.

Opposite page, bottom and above: A Patriot tactical air defence missile launcher of Battery E, 3rd Battalion, 43rd Air Defence Artillery, is deployed in the desert. This is an extremely effective anti-aircraft system, but it was not designed to shoot down SCUD missiles, even though at the time of 'Desert Storm' it was credited with doing so. Although Israel was not part of the Coalition, Patriot was deployed there after Iraq began launching SCUD missiles at the country. This was an attempt by the Iraqis to destablise the Coalition. Saddam Hussein's intention was to force Israel to enter the war and join the Coalition. Arab members of the Coalition, who could not be seen to side with Israel against another Arab nation, would then have to desert the alliance against Iraq.

Above: A soldier stakes down camouflage netting around a Patriot launcher. In the mid-1970s, during early development of the missile, a test firing programme achieved thirteen successes and only one failure. Full production commenced in 1982. The missile is stored and fired from its canister. Capable of supersonic speed, it is fitted with a high-explosive fragmentation warhead, and is able to outmanoeuvre and destroy any manned aircraft. Note the size the size of the system compared with the soldier.

Opposite page, top: Camouflage netting covers one of the trucks which houses the communications equipment for a Patriot air defence missile site.

Opposite page, bottom: An AN/MPQ-53 radar antenna unit for the Patriot air defence missile. The radar unit is a multifunctional, phased-array device which performs surveillance, tracking and guidance.

Above: Marine artillerymen set up their M198 155mm howitzer in preparation for a fire mission against Iraqi positions during Operation 'Desert Storm'. The 7-ton M198 is heavy and awkward to manhandle into position, exacerbated by the lack of an auxiliary power unit, which many such weapons have. Even so, the U.S. armed forces were content with these weapons, and they performed well during the fighting.

Opposite page, top and bottom: Marines of Company C, 1st Battalion, 2nd Marines after disembarking from Marine CH-46E Sea Knights belonging to 263 Squadron. The Sea Knight first entered service with the Marine Corps in 1964 and has been upgraded and improved over the years. It has a crew of three and can carry 25 troops or fifteen stretcher cases at a maximum speed of 150 miles per hour.

Above: A Marine Corps M1A1 Abrams equipped with a mine-clearing plow passes a knocked-out truck in an abandoned Iraqi position as the Marines advance into Kuwait. The Marine Corps used mostly the older M60 MBT during Operation Desert Storm, but they had 78 Abrams, some which were borrowed from Army stocks. The Abrams equipped the 2nd and 4th Marine Tank Battalions of the I Marine Expeditionary Force.

Opposite page, top and left: M1A1 Abrams MBTs of the 3rd Brigade, 1st Armored Division, VII Corps advance across the desert in northern Kuwait. U.S. 1st and 3rd Armored Divisions provided the main punching force of VII Corps as it rolled into Iraq which destroyed some 1,300 tanks during the battle to retake Kuwait.

Above: M1A1 Abrams MBTs of the 3rd Armored Division advancing during Operation 'Desert Storm'.

Right: A close-up view of the hole punched through the turret of a knocked-out Iraqi T-55 tank by an armour-piercing weapon.

Far right, top and bottom: Two T-55s knocked-out during Operation Gulf Storm. The bottom picture was taken on the 'Highway of Death' as the Iraqi forces tried to retreat back to Iraq. Note the graffiti painted on by Coalition troops.

Below: Marines man a TOW (Tube-launched, Optically-tracked, Wire-guided) anti-tank missile launcher mounted on top of a M998 HMMWV. The TOW's missile can penetrate 700mm of armour and has a range of 4,000 yards. Although it has been in service with the U.S. Army since 1970, and first saw combat during the Vietnam War, it has been continuously upgraded and it still proves to be a very effective weapon. The Iraqi armour at the battle for Khafji suffered heavy losses at the hands of U.S. Marines firing their TOW missiles.

Opposite page, top: An army marches on its stomach, and these marines seem to be eating well. The MRE (Meal Ready to Eat) was an unappetising pre-packaged combat ration that was intended to be eaten by G.I.s for up to ten days at a time. It was never intended to feed the men indefinitely. The U.S. Army used to have an excellent field food service but it had suffered during the reorganisation of its armed forces some fifteen years before. In Saudi Arabia there was not much of an alternative to the MREs, and G.I.s had to survive on one cooked meal and two MREs per day. But many an enterprising G.I. was soon bargaining with Allied troops in order to improve their rations.

Bottom right: Pensive troops of Company C, 1st Battalion, 187th Infantry, 101st Airborne Division (Air Assault) ('Screaming Eagles') aboard a C-130 Hercules transport plane during 'Desert Storm'. The 101st were to carry out the largest, and very successful, helicopter assault in military history during the course of the Gulf War.

Left: Seen here at the Iraqi Safwan Air Base, which was captured by the 1st Infantry Division, on the left are, General H. Norman Schwarzkopf, commander-in-chief, U.S. Central Command and Lieutenant General Prince Khalid bin Sultan, commander of Joint Forces in Saudi Arabia. Sitting opposite them are an Iraqi interpreter and two Iraqi Generals. With the Saddam-style mustache is General Ahmad, the Iraqi chief negotiator, and to his right General Mahmud. They are discussing the cease-fire conditions.

Bottom left: Protectively wrapped CH-47 Chinook helicopters, M1A1 Abrams MBTs and other armoured vehicles wait to be shipped back to the United States in the aftermath of the war.

Right: Troops of the U.S. Army's XVIII Airborne Corps ready to board a C-130 Hercules transport of the 1630th Tactical Airlift Wing for transit back to the United States. Most are wearing the desert camouflage BDUs but a few, on the left, can be seen wearing the woodland pattern camouflage BDUs.

Some of the U.S. generals who, with General Schwarzkopf, planned the war.

Left: Chairman of the Joint Chiefs of Staff, General Colin Powell.

Below left: General Alfred M. Gray, commandant of the Marine Corps.

Below: Brigadier General Steven Arnold, assistant chief of staff.

Right: Lieutenant General John J. Yeosock, commander of the 3rd U.S. Army and Army Forces Central Command.

Far right: Brigadier General John Liede, director of intelligence, U.S. Central Command.

Opposite page, bottom left: Major General James Starling, director of logistics and security assistance, U.S. Central Command.

Opposite page, bottom right: Major General Burton Moore, director of operations, U.S. Central Command.

Left: A military police woman from the Army's 284th Military Police Company controls a M60 machine-gun mounted on top of a M998 HMMWV. Coalition Forces are taking part in Operation 'Provide Comfort', an effort to aid Kurdish refugees who have fled Saddam Hussein's troops in northern Iraq shortly after the end of 'Desert Storm'. She is wearing the woodland pattern camouflage BDUs.

Right: A dental team from the 24th Marine Expeditionary Unit treat a Kurdish woman in a field hospital during Operation 'Provide Comfort'. They have removed their BDU jackets and are wearing service issue olive-drab cotton undershirts.

Left: G.I.s providing purified water for the Kurdish refugees during Operation 'Provide Comfort'. As northern Iraq has a much more temperate climate than the south, these G.I.s are wearing the woodland pattern camouflage BDUs. This is the standard uniform of the army and is worn both in the field and in garrison.

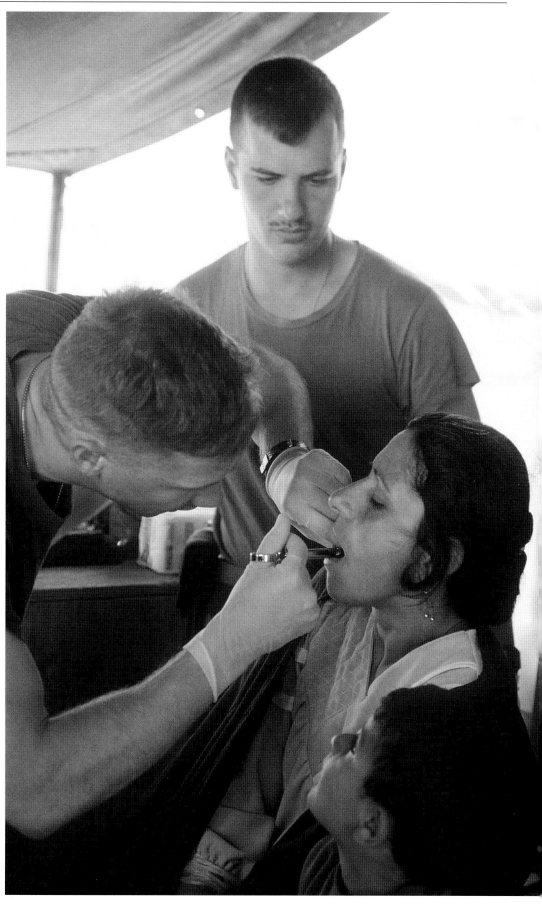

A victorious soldier of the 82nd Airborne Division is greeted by a loved one as he returns home to the United States from Operation 'Desert Storm'. He is still wearing his desert camouflage BDUs ('chocolate chips') and desert camouflage-covered 'Fritz' helmet, and he is still carrying his M16A2 rifle slung over his shoulder.